Discussion–Provoking Scripts for Teens

by
Don L. Sorenson, Ph.D.
with
David A. Nord

Copyright 2002
Educational Media Corporation®
PO Box 21311
Minneapolis, MN 55421-0311

763-781-0088
*www.**educationalmedia**.com*

ISBN 1-930572-16-6

Library of Congress Catalog No. 2002090981

Printing (last Digit)

9 8 7 6 5 4 3 2 1

Production Editor—
Don L. Sorenson, Ph.D.
Graphic Design—
Earl Sorenson

Introduction

Getting teenagers to talk is not difficult. They talk on the phone, the internet, with friends, and sometimes even with their parents. However, initiating a discussion that relates to some of the problems teens face can be difficult.

In this book we have provided some short scripts that relate to a number of situations encountered by teens. The purpose of these scripts is to provide a brief introduction to a subject that should result in a discussion by the audience. If you so desire, you can ask the actors to complete the scripts spontaneously or ask the audience to complete the scenarios.

We recommend that a certain amount of trust be present in the audience before the presentations are done. This can be accomplished by using some energizers and icebreakers that are available in a variety of books which are referenced on page 76. It helps if members of the audience or the class know the names of the other students, and perhaps, something significant about each person.

These scripts also can provide some necessary training for peer helpers who are going to be working with other students to help them deal with a variety of life problems.

The discussions that result from each presentation will vary according to the audience and the degree to which the actors get into the scripts. If you wish, you can encourage your actors to elaborate on the script and to personalize the dialog. Our purpose was to inspire a presentation, not to limit your students' creativity. While some situations may contain themes more appropriate for older teens, an effort was made to use language that would be acceptable to teens of all ages.

Little or no preparation is required to turn the scripts into effective dramatic presentations. The list of subjects covered is by no means exhaustive. Our goal was to stimulate thinking and to encourage the use of scripts to focus discussions on important teen issues.

Discussion questions and some notes on the concepts presented follow each script.

Table of Contents

Don L. Sorenson, Ph.D. with David A. Nord

Section I
Among Friends

1   **What are Friends For?**

Subject: Copying homework

Setting: A school hallway before the first hour class

Props: Homework folder for Melissa, a sign that says "Locker," and a clock face with moveable hands

Cast: Steve, Melissa, Connie, and a stage hand

Synopsis: Steve didn't get his homework done last night, so he asked Melissa if he could borrow hers so he would have a sample of the writeup to follow. He promises to return it to Melissa after study hall.

(A stage hand comes out and hangs a sign that says "Locker," hangs a clock, and sets the hands to 8:00.)

Steve   Can I ask a favor?

Melissa   Sure. What is it?

Steve   Did you get yesterday's ex–periment written up yet?

Melissa   Yep. I did it last night.

Steve   I had to take care of my little brother last night. He was really being a pain. I was planning to get it done after he went to bed, but I was too tired.

Melissa   You know we have to hand it in fourth hour.

Steve   I know. I was hoping you would let me see your writeup. I could finish mine during study hall if I had something to follow.

Melissa   Well, I suppose I could let you look at it, just to give you an idea of what to write, but I have to have it back before fourth hour. *(She hands her homework folder to Steve.)*

Steve   Great! I'll see you here by your locker at the end of third hour at 10:30.

Melissa   Okay. See you then.
              (A stage hand comes out and changes the clock hands to 10:30.)

Melissa   Where is he?

Connie   Who?

Melissa   Steve. He was supposed to meet me here at 10:30, but he's not here. It's real impor–tant.

Connie   I don't think he is going to make it. I saw him in study hall. He told the teacher he wasn't feeling well and went to the nurse's office. I think he went home.

Melissa   Great! Now what am I going to do? He has my science report and it is due next hour. I'm really in trouble now.

Connie   Why did Steve have it in the first place?

Melissa   I let him look at it because he needed some ideas for his writeup. Now I won't be able to turn my report in on time. I was just trying to help him. What am I going to do?

Processing Questions

1. Did Steve have a valid excuse for not getting his homework done?

2. If you suspect that what you are doing is not quite right, what should you do?

3. What could Melissa have said to Steve to avoid the problem that occurred later?

4. Is it cheating just to "look at" someone else's homework to get an idea of how to do yours?

5. Melissa trusted Steve to return her homework before fourth hour. What conditions need to be present for you to trust someone?

6. Sometimes the unexpected happens. What other things could have happened to keep Steve from returning the homework on time?

7. What would keep Melissa from simply explaining to her teacher what happened?

Discussion Notes

Melissa chose to loan her homework to Steve so he would have an "example to follow" while doing his own writeup. The differences between *modeling* and *copying* should be explored. *Plagiarism* should be defined. You might also wish to cover the use of proper references when using material from other sources.

Melissa took a risk when she trusted Steve to return something that was valuable to her. Discuss what it feels like when you put yourself at risk by lending something that is valuable to someone else.

You reduce the level of risk–taking as you increase the level of trust that exists between two people. Melissa probably felt intimidated by Steve. You might present some assertiveness strategies that Melissa could have used to politely say no to Steve's request.

2 Partners?

Subject	Shirking responsibility
Setting	A gathering place after school
Props	Folder containing a science project
Cast	Josh and Monica
Synopsis	Josh is having trouble getting Monica to do her share of a science project. Monica puts everything else ahead of working with Josh. She is willing to have him do all of the work since he is so capable and she is not.

Josh I thought you agreed to be my partner on this science project.

Monica I did.

Josh But, I almost have it done and you haven't done anything.

Monica I told you to tell me when you wanted help, but you haven't even called me.

Josh I talked to you after class yesterday. You said you didn't have any time this weekend, so I worked on it last night.

Monica Well, Mike asked me to go skiing with him this weekend. I haven't been skiing all winter.

Josh Neither have I. This project is due next Wednesday. I've had to give up some things I like to do. I guess I thought when I agreed to partner with you, that you would be willing to do some of the work.

Monica I will; just not this weekend.

Josh Well, how about Monday night?

Monica Monday night.... I can't. Our volleyball team meets on Monday night.

Josh Can't you skip it just once?

Monica No. I'm captain of the team and I have to be there.

Josh Well, what about Tuesday night? But, I hate to wait until the last minute to get it done.

Monica I don't know of anything on Tuesday night. I guess we could do it then.

Josh You guess? And if something more important comes up Tuesday night, then I'll have to finish it alone, right?

Monica I thought you said you had it almost done?

Josh And I thought you said you would help. Is this your idea of helping?

Monica You're so good in science. I just knew I could count on you to get me through this. You really don't need my help.

Josh So, is this what you think "being a partner" means?

Processing Questions

1. What qualities do you look for in someone with whom you have to work?

2. Is it a good idea to work with a friend, or would it be better to pair up with someone else?

3. If you have something to accomplish, do you prefer to get it done right now or would you rather wait until closer to the time it is due?

4. If you have too many obligations, how do you set your priorities?

5. If people say they will "try," how should you interpret that message?

6. When you are with your friends, are you a leader or a follower?

7. On what types of projects do you feel most comfortable taking the lead?

Discussion Notes

We often find out the most about the qualities of others when we work with them. People who agree to work together on projects often have differing opinions of what that means. Usually someone has to take the leadership, letting others know what is expected. When we say we will try, it usually means we anticipate failure. Make sure your expectations of others are clearly stated before going into a work relationship. Partnerships need to be renegotiated from time to time as you learn more about the other person's work habits.

3   **Lunchroom Musical Chairs**

Subject	New student rejected
Setting	A table for four in the school lunchroom. Three guys are sitting eating their lunches. There is room for one more person.
Props	Table, four chairs, four lunch trays
Cast	Dave, Brad, Scott, and Jason
Synopsis	A new student is looking for a place to sit in the lunchroom. He approaches a group where there is an empty seat, asking permission to join them.

Dave   What did you and Doris do last night?

Brad   Caught the new movie at the Heights.

Scott   What did you guys do afterwards?

Brad   The usual. We drove around a little. There wasn't much happening last night.

Jason   (*walks up to the table with his tray*) Mind if I sit here?

Dave   Actually, we do. That's Mike's spot.

Jason   I don't see his name on it.

Brad   Well, that's where he sits every day.

Jason   I don't see any place else to sit.

Dave   Is that our problem?

Jason   I just thought it would be okay if I sat here.

Brad   Well, it isn't.

Dave   Besides, we don't even know you.

Jason   Maybe I'm worth getting to know.

Scott   So what's to know? Are you new here?

Jason   I've been here about a week. I transferred from Central High. It's kind of tough to get new friends. Everybody seems to already have their groups. What's a new guy supposed to do?

Processing Questions

1. What was your first impression of Jason?
2. Why did Jason ask permission to sit down?
3. Do you sit in the same place each day at lunch?
4. How would your group of friends have reacted to someone like Jason?
5. What could Jason have said to have received a better wel–come?
6. Is it difficult for transfer students to "find their places" in a new school?
7. What do we do at our school to ease the tension for new students?

Discussion Notes

One Florida counselor from a school with a large number of transfer students reported that many new students go at least a week without eating lunch for fear of not sitting in the right place or with the right group. Discussing what the situation is in your school should lead to some suggestions for ways to help new students to feel welcome.

Here is an excellent project for students in a peer helper pro–gram. One service that can be provided to new students is to pair them with peer helpers who provide a personal orientation to the school, including an invitation to sit with them at lunch.

4   **Second Thoughts**

Subject	Wrong prom date
Setting	Any place for gathering after school
Props	None required
Cast	Jean and Gloria
Synopsis	Jean regrets accepting an invitation to the prom. She had hoped another boy would invite her. She is unhappy with her decision and hopes there is something she can do to be able to go with the boy she prefers.

Jean   Guess who asked me to go to the prom?

Gloria   I don't know. Who?

Jean   Ryan Turner.

Gloria   Ryan? Wow! That's great! When did he ask you?

Jean   At lunch.

Gloria   How did he ask you?

Jean   He just asked me if I had a date for the prom. Like an idiot, I said no. So then he asked me if I'd go with him. What was I supposed to say?

Gloria   Well, you were supposed to say yes.

Jean   Yeah, but I'm not sure I want to go with him.

Gloria   Why not? He's cute.

Jean   I was kind of hoping that someone else was going to get around to asking me.

Gloria   Anybody I know?

Jean   You might. He's in my sixth hour class. I kind of like him. The other day I saw him star–ing at me across the room, and yesterday he walked to class with me. I get the feeling that he likes me, but he won't say anything.

Gloria   What's his name?

Jean   Gary Fisher.

Gloria   Well, I guess it is a little late to do anything about the prom now. It's only two weeks away and you've already told Ryan that you'd go with him.

Jean   I know. What should I do?

Processing Questions

1. If you change your mind about an invitation, how can you let that person know?
2. Can you have a good time at a party with someone that you have "luke warm" feelings about?
3. If you are in doubt, how can you buy a little more time to think about something before making a decision?
4. How do you let someone know that you care about that person?
5. Would you rather do things socially with a group of friends or with a single person?
6. What are some fun things to do on a first date with someone?
7. What does the following saying mean? "To not decide is to decide."

Discussion Notes

Sometimes choices are made prematurely, causing what we call "cognitive dissonance" about the choice–regret that we have made the choice and wishing that we could do something to change it. Choice making should follow a specific procedure to avoid regretting our decisions. We should first clearly identify the decision to be made, list the alternatives available, and the consequences of choosing each. Take time to think it through before making and announcing our decision, because once our decision is made, a new direction for our life has been taken. Decision making is an important process and it should be done properly.

5   He's not Heavy....

Subject	Brotherly put downs
Setting	A place where two friends can talk
Props	None required
Cast	Karl and Ryan
Synopsis	Karl's brother is always putting him down when he is with his friends. He doesn't think his brother cares how the put downs make him feel.

Karl   I get so mad sometimes. I could kill him.

Ryan   Why? What's your brother done this time?

Karl   It's not what he's done, it's what he said.

Ryan   Which was?

Karl   When he's with his friends, he's always got to put me down. He thinks he is so tough when they're around. He calls me names like faggot and fairy. He treats me like crap.

Ryan   I thought you two got along?

Karl   Well, we do most of the time. He just changes when he's with his friends. I just hate it when that happens.

Ryan   Why don't you tell your mom or dad?

Karl   What good would that do? He'd just have some more names to call me, like "mama's boy" or "crybaby." Besides, what would my mom or dad do?

Ryan   Have you tried talking to him? Letting him know how it feels when he calls you names?

Karl   Why would he care how I feel? I guess he thinks I'm not supposed to have feelings.

Ryan   What do you mean?

Karl   He thinks it's only girls who have feelings. He pretends like nothing affects him. He laughs in movies, even at the sad stuff. He doesn't want anyone to really get close to him.

Ryan   I know he has feelings. He just doesn't want to show them.

Karl   What's he afraid of?

Processing Questions

1. Do you notice that a brother or friend treats you differently when certain others are present?
2. What are some of the positive experiences that you share with a sibling?
3. Do you treat older brothers and sisters differently than you treat younger ones?
4. When do you experience the most friction with a brother or sister?
5. How difficult is it for you to talk to your siblings?
6. Are you competing with a brother or sister for a parent's attention or affection?
7. How can you tell another what that person has done to hurt your feelings?
8. Do you generally have positive feelings toward your brothers and sisters?

Discussion Notes

Siblings generally share the largest portion of your life as you grow up. You share the same parents, home, and intimate experiences. As you get older and become more involved with out–side acquaintances, your siblings take more of a back seat. You attempt to assert your independence from home and family, sometimes putting down family members in front of new friends. Independence does not always have to come at the expense of the feelings of family members. Being able to share your feelings with family members helps to keep those relation-ships on positive footings.

6   Who's Disgusting?

Subject   Put downs

Setting   Any place where students gather

Props   None required

Cast   Paul, Carlos, Liz, Amy, and Kathy (*Kathy is on the heavy side. You might accomplish this with padding rather than by using type casting.*)

Synopsis   Paul and Carlos decide to shower Kathy with put downs. Later, Liz and Amy give Carlos a taste of his own medicine.

Paul   Hey, saddle bags. What did you have for lunch. The whole cow?

Carlos You're so fat. I tried to swerve around you, and I ran out of gas.

Kathy   Why do you guys always make fun of me?

Paul   Because you're an easy target.

Carlos You're disgusting to look at.

Kathy   I can't help the way I look. I have an eating disorder. I'm trying to lose weight, but it isn't easy.

Carlos Yeah, you are on a see food diet–you see food and you eat it.

Kathy   Stuff like that doesn't help at all. I feel bad enough about my condition without having you guys rubbing it in all time. Can't you just say something nice once in a while?

Paul   Sorry, can't do that.

(Later that day, Carlos meets up with Liz and Amy.)

Liz   Hey, Carlos. You are so stupid that you would climb over a glass wall to see what is on the other side.

Amy   You're so dumb. I bet you think Cherrios are donut seeds.

Carlos No I wouldn't.

Liz   You're so dumb that it takes you two hours to watch "60 Minutes."

Amy   You're so stupid you tripped over a cordless phone.

Carlos What did I ever do to you?

Liz   Nothing. You are just so dense. You make it so easy.

Carlos Don't you think I have any feelings?

Processing Questions

1. What reasons do people use for putting down others?
2. What types of people are targets of your put downs?
3. What types of people offend you?
4. Is it true that some people are not responsible for how they look, i.e., eating disorders?
5. Are you fearful of people you do not know?
6. Have you ever been the target of put downs? If so, how did you feel?
7. Some people say that put downs are clumsy attempts to get acquainted with someone else. Do you see any truth in that statement?
8. What do you do to stop yourself from putting down others?

Discussion Notes

For a democratic society, we appear to have a well–defined pecking order that results in put downs being heaped upon those we see as inferior or different from ourselves. We amuse our peers by coming up with clever statements that are deliv–ered at the expense of others. While the use of put downs begins early in our social lives, it continues into the teenage years, inflicting great pain on the victims. Fear of the unknown is often given as the reason why we try to distance ourselves from those whom we perceive as different from ourselves. One way to keep that distance is to put others down. It is hard to get close to someone who inflicts hurt on us.

7   Dividing the Tab

Subject	Being fair
Setting	A restaurant with waiter service
Props	Restaurant table, waiter's bill, paper, and pencil
Cast	Waiter and three student customers, Shane, Matt, and Justin
Synopsis	After enjoying a meal together, Shane, Matt, and Justin are presented with the bill. Matt tries to divide up the expenses, but Justin suggests that it be divided evenly. Shane objects because he did not order as much food as the others.

Waiter Is there anything else I can get you?

Shane Nope. I guess we're ready for the bill.

Waiter Here you are, guys. You can pay me when you are ready.

Matt *(picking up the bill)* All right, let's see. Justin, you had a coke, double cheeseburger, fries, and shake. I had chicken fingers, fries, milk, and a couple of cookies. Shane. Looks like you just had a hamburger and a coke.

Justin Why don't we just divide it evenly? That'll save all the math hassles.

Matt Sounds good to me.

Shane That's not fair. I only had a hamburger and a coke. Your share is twice as much as mine. Why should I have to pay for some of your food?

Justin So, it's not our fault that you didn't order more.

Shane Well, maybe I just wasn't that hungry.

Matt What's the big deal, Shane? It's just a couple of bucks.

Shane The big deal is I don't think it's fair. I ordered less than you, so I should pay less than you guys do.

Justin Who says life is fair?

Shane Well, I thought my friends were fair. Maybe I would have liked to have french fries, a malt or some cookies, and just couldn't afford it.

Matt So what are you saying–you're broke?

Shane I didn't say that. I said maybe the reason I didn't order as much as you guys did was I didn't have enough money to pay for it.

Justin Don't you have enough money to pay a third of the bill?

Shane Maybe... maybe not. That's not the problem. The problem is I don't want to pay for food that I didn't eat.

Matt So, what should we do?

Processing Questions

1. What assumptions did Bill make when he suggested that the bill be divided evenly?
2. What is unfair about dividing a bill evenly?
3. Do you think Shane was short of money?
4. Why do some diners always ask for separate checks?
5. When dining with others, when should the method of payment be discussed?
6. Should life be fair?
7. What things appear to be unfair in your life?

Discussion Notes

Friendships often are stressed by things that are said and done that appear to be unfair. While it has been said that "life is unfair," we still are unhappy when our friends and family members do not treat us fairly. You might want to identify other situations that your students have experienced that they perceive to be unfair, and discuss ways they would have preferred to have been treated.

Also, it is helpful to provide a model for giving feedback to someone who has treated you unfairly without becoming obnoxious in the process. The "I message" model: tell persons how a specific behavior has made you feel, and what action you–not they–are prompted to do as a result. Example: "You know, Bill, when you suggested that we split the bill evenly, it angered me that you didn't perceive that my share of the bill should have been less than yours or Matt's, and I doubt whether I would be willing to go out with you again."

Don L. Sorenson, Ph.D. with David A. Nord

8 Growing Apart

Subject   Fading friendship
Setting   Anywhere friends gather after school
Props   None required
Cast   Marlana and Julia
Synopsis   Longtime friends discover they are growing apart. They no longer share mutual activities.

Marlana   Do you remember when we were in kindergarten?

Julia   Yeah, what about it?

Marlana   We promised to be friends forever.

Julia   And we are...

Marlana   It just seems that things are changing.

Julia   What do you mean?

Marlana   We don't do as many things together as we used to.

Julia   Like what?

Marlana   You used to come over and we would just spend time together. Now it seems like we always have to have something planned.

Julia   Well, we're busier now.

Marlana   Yeah, but we are busier with different things. You seem to be doing more things with others than you do with me.

Julia   Maybe it's because you don't always want to do what I'm doing.

Marlana   You're into sports and I just want to have fun.

Julia   Sports are fun. Especially when you get good at them and win.

Marlana   That's too much work. It isn't fun when you have to practice all the time.

Julia   I guess we are growing apart. I like competition, but it appears that doesn't float your boat.

Marlana   There must be something that we still have in common.

Julia   We're still friends.

Marlana   But, friends do things together. We used to do a lot of things together.

Julia   Times change and people do too. Maybe it is time to move on. What do you think?

Processing Questions

1. What has happened to some of your friendships from grade school?
2. What kinds of things do you like to do with your friends?
3. What conditions make for good friendships?
4. How do you go about making friends with someone you have just met?
5. How would you describe your friends?
6. How would your friends describe you?
7. Is there anything that has changed about you that you don't like?
8. Are you comfortable having a few friends, or is it important for you to have many friends?

Discussion Notes

Although we often take them for granted, our friends are very important. As we get older, we spend less time with our families and more time with our friends. Our first friends usually lived close by so we could spend time with them easily. As our worlds expand, so does the number of people from which we can choose our friends. As our interests change, our preferences for people with whom to spend our time also changes. It is important for us to know what we value in a friend, and to choose people that possess deep qualities.

Section II
Working to Please

9 **Too Good to be True**

Subject   Practice vs. fun

Setting   School music room

Props   Erik, Julian, and Nikki

Cast   Musical instrument, case, or music stand

Synopsis   Two young musicians share their enthusiasm for their accomplishments. Nikki tries to get Julian to cut practice and have a little fun.

Erik I'm really looking forward to this weekend.

Julian Yeah, me too. This will be the first time I can play my com-position in public.

Erik My mom says that I will be the youngest bassoon player in the program.

Julian It's worth practicing every day to play at the Orpheum.

Erik I get picked on sometimes for spending so much time prac-ticing, but I really enjoy it.

Julian How did you happen to choose the bassoon?

Erik My band director said it was a real difficult instrument. I knew it would be a challenge.

Julian Was it?

Erik At first. But, now it comes easy. My band director says I am "a natural."

Julian My piano teachers says that I have what it takes to be a great composer. I just hear melodies in my head and I have to write them down.

Nikki Hi, Julian.

Julian Hi, Nikki.

Erik Hello, Nikki.

Nikki Oh yeah, you too, Erik. Hey, Julian. Can you help me with my math after school? Then maybe we could go over to Micky D's after we're done.

Erik Don't forget you have to prac-tice after school, Julian.

Nikki Come on. You practice enough. Besides, I need help.

Julian But, Nikki. I have a big concert coming up this weekend and I want to do my best.

Nikki Is that piano the only thing in your life? You act like you are married to it.

Julian The piano is very important to me. I am good at it, and I want to be the best.

Nikki There is more to life than music. Why don't you ever want to have any fun?

Julian I am having fun. I wish you would appreciate how I feel about my music.

Nikki I appreciate your music, but I wish you had some time for other things once in a while.

Julian Like what, for instance?

Processing Questions

1. Is there something that you enjoy doing that takes a lot of practice?

2. Are you willing to take on challenges, or do you prefer to do things that are simple and easy to accomplish?

3. Do some people just have natural ability to do some things, or can we all learn if we want to?

4. Are you easily distracted when you have a difficult task to do?

5. Do you get pleasure just from accomplishing something difficult?

6. What do you wish you could be able to do, but haven't committed the time to learn?

7. What does "delayed gratification" mean?

Discussion Notes

Acquiring certain skills requires a commitment to lots of practice. While some people may appear to be naturally gifted, a commitment to practice is necessary to polish and hone skills sufficiently to be a performer or a winner. Dedication and commitment sometimes are challenged by distractions. Those who commit to something often are labeled "nerds" because of their single-mindedness. The maturity to delay gratification–to wait for the rewards–is essential to committing time to long regimens of practice.

10   Late Nights?

Subject	Sleeping in class
Setting	A classroom, first hour in the day
Props	2 chairs and 2 desks
Cast	Kirk, Julie, and a teacher
Synopsis	Kirk's teacher confronts him when he has his head down on his desk. Kirk is accused of partying and not getting his homework done. He tells the teacher that he has heavy work responsibilities outside of school and that is why he is tired.

Teacher Kirk, wake up!

Kirk What? Oh, I'm sorry.

Teacher Rough night last night, Kirk?

Kirk No. I just went to bed. I was pretty tired.

Teacher Do you expect me to believe that? I'll bet you probably were partying last night.

Kirk I never have time to party.

Teacher Oh, come on. Tell me another one. What teenage boy doesn't party occasionally?

Kirk I don't.

Julie Why are you picking on him?

Teacher I'm not picking on him. I just don't appreciate it when a student sleeps in class.

Kirk I'm sorry. It won't happen again.

Teacher Kirk, do you have your home-work done?

Kirk I wasn't able to finish it last night. I'll get it done in study hall this afternoon.

Teacher But, it was due this morning.

Julie Can't you give him a break?

Teacher A deadline is a deadline. By the way, why couldn't you get it done, Kirk?

Kirk I have to get up at 5:00 a.m. to help my dad with the chores. When I get home from school, I've got those chores to do again. After supper, I am just too tired to study. How am I supposed to do it all?

Processing Questions

1. What penalty should be imposed when a deadline is missed?
2. How many hours do you think the average student should study each day?
3. How many hours per week should a student be able to work and still meet school obligations?
4. How many hours of sleep are necessary for the average teenager?
5. If you have too many responsibilities, how do you set your priorities?
6. What considerations should teachers make for students who have to work?
7. Should teenagers have a curfew on weekday nights?
8. Would students do better if classes didn't start so early in the morning?

Discussion Notes

In addition to full days in school, many teenagers have outside work assignments. Adding homework requirements, it is not uncommon for them to be stressed out or tired. Teachers expect their students to come to school ready to learn and they are disappointed when they are less than responsive in class. How much consideration should be given by teachers to students' outside work loads? Teachers believe the first priority should be to school. Sports and recreation are usually considered to be farther down the list. Even outside work is usually secondary to getting an education. But, how about responsibilities to the family? Not all students work just to pay for the luxury of owning their own car. With single parent families, out of work parents, and family illnesses, some students are required to contribute financially to the family.

11   I'd Rather Drop Out

Subject	Poor grades
Setting	Family home, probably around the kitchen table
Props	Report card
Cast	Mom, Dad, and son, Hue
Synopsis	Hue brings home his report card with some low grades. His dad blames his part time job for his poor school performance. Hue says he is learning more on the job than he is in school. His solution to the problem is to drop out of school and work full time.

Mom I don't like what I am seeing on your report card.

Hue What's wrong? I'm still pass-ing.

Mom Barely. I don't consider Ds and one C passing. You've got to do better.

Hue I'm trying, but by the time I get done with work, I'm pretty tired. Besides, I don't really like my biology teacher. He doesn't explain things very well.

(Dad enters the room.)

Dad Are you talking about that report card?

Hue Yeah.

Dad Pretty bad, kid. Something has got to change.

Hue Like what?

Dad I told you that if I let you get that job, you would have to keep your grades up.

Hue My job has nothing to do with it. I like my job. I'm learning a lot. School sucks, that's all.

Mom What's wrong with school? You were doing well last year. What's happened?

Hue I'm just not learning any-thing useful. At work, I learn practical things that I can use and I feel like I'm some-body. At school, well, its just boring. I'll never use any of that stuff. Why can't I just drop out and work full time?

Processing Questions

1. Could working part time be affecting Hue's school work?
2. Hue's dad feels that the major change in Hue's life from last year was the addition of a part time job. What else might have changed to contribute to his lower grades?
3. What limits should be placed on employment during the school week?
4. Do your parents have the same perception as you do as to what constitutes "passing" grades?
5. How much time each week should be devoted to homework to keep your grades up?
6. What things are you asked to learn in school that appear to have no practical value?
7. What reasons could you give Hue for staying in school through high school?
8. Parents and teachers often punish their children for poor grades by denying them access to something they do well (i.e., sports, work). How do you feel about this practice?

Discussion Notes

Working part time often has a great deal more appeal than the usual school routine. Doing something that appears to be useful, earning money, and gaining some sense of responsibility are some of the positives associated with working. Classes and school work have to compete for attention and effort. While the short term gains of part time work seem to overshadow the delayed gratification that comes with a high school diploma, most students have been told about the long term benefits of graduating.

Students need to have a personal appreciation for the long term rewards that await them if they are going to have the tenacity to stick with their school work and forgo the short term gratifications.

You can broaden this discussion, if you wish, to those who see teenage parenting as another way to rush into the adult world for the rewards for which they perceive they cannot wait.

12   Like Father...

Subject	Career choices
Setting	Outside Ben's family store
Props	Sign for the front of the store
Cast	Ben and Ben's father
Synopsis	Ben's father holds a lifelong dream to have his son join him in the business. Even though he has helped his dad in the store for several years, Ben has different ambitions.

Dad I can't wait to add the words "and son" to that sign. Since the day you were born I have been looking forward to having you work with me here in the store.

Ben Dad, I have been working with you since I was twelve.

Dad You know what I mean. Having you take over some of the management responsibilities. We'd be partners.

Ben I don't know how to say this, Dad, but I really wasn't planning to work in the store forever.

Dad What do you mean?

Ben Dad, I enjoy drawing. I was hoping to go to a technical college to learn to become a commercial artist.

Dad Why would you want to waste your money on college when you can have a great job working with me that would pay just as good as an artist?

Ben But, Dad, I just don't picture myself working in this store five years from now when I really want be an artist working for a publisher.

Dad I've spent all of my life planning for the day you would take over. What will happen to the store when I am no longer able to manage it?

Ben I guess you will probably have to sell it .

Dad Sell it! Are you crazy? I've had this store for twenty years and I'm not about to sell it.

Ben Well, I guess what happens to the store is really your problem, not mine. I have my own life to live.

Dad My mistake. I always thought you wanted to be a partner someday. I guess all my efforts to build this business have been for nothing. Where did I go wrong?

Processing Questions

1. Is it fair for a parent to expect a child to continue in the family business?

2. Do your parents have any responsibility for helping you to choose your own career? Lifestyle?

3. Do you have some ambitions for your life that your parents do not share?

4. What responsibilities do parents have to help their children reach their goals?

5. Are your parents supportive of your need for independence?

6. Will you expect any financial support from your parents after you graduate from high school?

7. Are there some things that you do that are in direct rebellion with your parents?

8. What goals would you have for your children when they grow up?

Discussion Notes

Parents bring their children into the world, raising them through adolescence, and hope that they will become successful adults. Many of their own ambitions and drives are centered on helping their children to do well. Parents who have spent a lifetime raising their children and building their businesses cannot help but dream that someday their children will be their adult part–ners–in life, and perhaps, even in a business. Many parents do recognize, however, that their children are unique individuals and have different interests than their own. Separating their personal goals from those of their children requires that they have broad goals for their children, not specific ones. A discus–sion of what goals parents should have for their children could be very productive.

13   Is There Life After High School?

Subject   College selection

Setting   Any place friends gather, table and chairs

Props   College applications

Cast   Yumi, Carrie, and Meg

Synopsis   Yumi is having trouble getting started applying to colleges. She doesn't appear to have enough motivation to do what it takes to get accepted in a college.

Yumi   I know I should get some applications filled out, but I just can't seem to get motivated about going to college.

Carrie   I don't know why we have to be in such a hurry.

Meg   My dad says that if you want to have the best chance of getting in, you should get your applications in early.

Carrie   I can't even imagine graduating from high school, and we are supposed to know where we want to go to college.

Yumi   It seems like such a hassle. Why can't we wait a little longer? I'm not even sure I want to go to college.

Meg   But, if you wait too long, then the only college you can get into will be a community college.

Carrie   A community college wouldn't be so bad. I could live at home and be with my friends.

Meg   Some of your friends won't be at home, though. Some of us already have our applications done. We are planning to go away to college.

Yumi   I'll probably still be around, Carrie. I kind of like working at Target. I'll probably be a shift manager by the time I graduate. Besides, I'm kind of tired of the studying hassle. I just want to make some money, shop with my friends, and go to a party once in a while.

Carrie   That sounds kind of like a "dead end," Yumi. I think I want something more out of life. I guess I really want to go to college. I just can't seem to get into the process of applying.

Meg   Maybe you need something or someone to motivate you.

Carrie   What do you mean?

Meg   Well, if you are having trouble getting started on the application process, maybe you need more motivation.

Carrie   Like what?

Meg   I'm not sure. Let's talk about it a little more. What do you really want out of life? Which long range goals can best be fulfilled with a college education?

Processing Questions

1. Why is it so important to make post high school plans early?
2. What questions should you be asking your parents about college?
3. Is where you go to college that important? Why?
4. Do you have to know what you are going to major in to choose a college?
5. What are some of the advantages of going to a community college? Technical college?
6. In visiting perspective colleges, what should you look for on the campus?
7. Besides going to college, what other options do you have after high school graduation?
8. How do you plan to finance your post high school education?

Discussion Notes

With high school graduation over a year away, few students can focus on taking some preliminary steps toward planning "life after high school." Parents often feel they are "pushing" their children to make decisions they are not prepared to make. Preliminary discussions regarding post high school plans should begin before the pressure to decide is upon them. A discussion as to the timeline for making those decisions should result in establishing a calendar and a "decision to make when" list.

14   I'm Not Happy

Subjects	Teen depression
Setting	Ashley's bedroom
Props	Non required
Cast	Ashley and Lisa
Synopsis	Ashley is suffering from depression and cannot identify the cause. Her dad thinks it is just a phase and that she will grow out of it. Her mom won't go against her dad.

Ashley   I don't know what causes it. People keep asking me what's wrong. I can't tell them. I'm just feeling down all the time.

Lisa   You really don't know what's causing it?

Ashley   No. If I knew, maybe I could do something about it.

Lisa   It must be frustrating.

Ashley   It is. I keep hoping that some-one can help me figure out what's going on.

Lisa   Have you talked to someone like a doctor?

Ashley   The only way my parents would take me to a doctor is if I broke a bone or some-thing. They don't believe that doctors can help with "men-tal" problems.

Lisa   Maybe it's not "mental." There could be something like a chemical imbalance that is causing it–or maybe even a tumor.

Ashley   I did tell my parents that I thought there was something wrong with me.

Lisa   And what did they say?

Ashley   My dad thought it was just a phase I was going through. He said I would grow out of it.

Lisa   Well, what about your mom?

Ashley   She wouldn't go against my dad. I think she believes it's just a teenager thing.

Lisa   Even though your parents don't seem too concerned, you are still worried and wish you could do something about this, right?

Ashley   That's right, Lisa, my grades are good; there's no real prob-lems at home; I don't have boyfriend problems–nobody's picking on me. I just feel depressed. I don't sleep well or have much of an appetite.

Lisa   I can feel your desperation. I wish I could help. What would you like me to do?

Processing Questions

1. Is it possible to be depressed and not be able to identify the cause or reason?

2. Is depression something that you will more than likely grow out of?

3. Why do some people view psychological problems differently than medical ones?

4. Why is it hard to admit that someone in our family has problems?

5. How can friends help friends who are depressed?

6. Are there any medications that might help someone who is depressed?

7. If someone confides in you that he or she is experiencing depression, should you feel responsible to tell an adult?

Discussion Notes

Depression can be brought on by obvious causes, or it can be difficult, if not impossible, to identify a cause. Chemical imbalances can be treated with medicines; counseling can help individuals to learn alternative ways of coping with frustrations in life. Teenage depression can be serious, and often contributes to suicide attempts. It should not be ignored by friends, family, or teachers. Knowing what to do to help those who are experiencing depression can be lifesaving. Discuss the signs of depression and appropriate steps to take to get the person to seek professional help.

15   Ouch, that Hurts!

Subject   Physical contact

Setting   After school anywhere

Props   None required

Cast   Marvin and Chuck

Synopsis   Chuck gives Marvin a light punch to the arm and discovers that Marvin doesn't like any form of touching. Chuck learns that Marvin is afraid of any displays of physical affection.

Marvin   Hey! Stop! Quit hitting me.

Chuck   You're no fun.

Marvin   I just don't like anybody hitting me in the arm for no reason.

Chuck   I was just playing around.

Marvin   Well, I don't like it.

Chuck   Come on! My brothers and I are always hitting each other for fun.

Marvin   Well, I don't have any brothers. But, if I did, I wouldn't want them punching and hitting me.

Chuck   It's just our way of showing we care. We don't go around hugging and that kind of stuff, but we definitely mix it up a lot.

Marvin   My dad used to hit me a lot... especially when he was drunk.

Chuck   Did he hurt you?

Marvin   Sure. It didn't feel good to be knocked around—and for no reason at all.

Chuck   Did your dad ever hug you, or horse around with you?

Marvin   I can't remember him ever touching me, except to hit me when he was angry.

Chuck   How about your mom? Doesn't she hold you or give you a hug once in a while?

Marvin   No. My sister was born a couple of years after me. She was always sick. My mom never really had much time for me. It seemed like I was always in the way.

Chuck   So, are you close to anyone? Physically, I mean.

Marvin   I guess not. I've never thought much about it.

Chuck   I don't think I could handle that. I need to know someone cares enough about me to touch me.

Marvin   Yeah, but if the only way you get touched hurts, then who needs that?

Chuck   I've heard that some people would rather get hit once in a while than to be neglected all together.

Marvin   Well, not me.

Chuck But, deep down, wouldn't you like to have a close enough relationship to someone where you would feel comfortable enough to be touched?

Marvin Hey, I'm not gay, man.

Chuck Are you afraid that if you open up to a few punches from your friends, someone would think you were gay?

Processing Questions

1. Why is it so difficult for some people to let others touch them?

2. Do we learn to appreciate being touched?

3. What favorite physical activity do you like to do with others?

4. Can fears about touching affect our ability to be intimate with a person we care about?

5. Do people who allow others to physically abuse them do it because they would rather be beaten than neglected?

6. Are you concerned that you might do something to cause others to think you were gay?

7. Did a person who is gay make that choice, or did it just happen?

8. How do you show friends of the same sex that you care about them?

Discussion Notes

We all need physical stimulation–contact from other human beings. Deprived of it as a child, we might either try to make up for it by excessive physical contact or we might avoid it because we fear what we do not know. Intimacy requires that we are comfortable with physical contact. Society has placed certain restrictions on what types of physical contact we can show in public without being labeled as different, gay, or "mental." Individuals should feel comfortable discussing the types of physical contact they prefer, and the ones that they do not want. Communication helps people to find each other so they can satisfy mutual needs.

16   It Couldn't Happen to Me

Subject   Sexually-transmitted infections
Setting   Doctor's examining room
Props   Table
Cast   Sally and her doctor
Synopsis   Sally learns she has contracted a sexually-transmitted infection and is afraid to tell her parents.

Sally   Do you have to tell my parents?

Doctor No, I am not required by law to inform them. But, don't you think it would be best if you told them?

Sally   My dad would kill me. And my mom—well, I don't want to hurt her.

Doctor They might be more understanding than you think.

Sally   I don't think so. My brother got his girlfriend pregnant when he was a senior. They almost disowned him. He doesn't come around much any more.

Doctor You are going to need to confide in someone. There are some things you need to talk about with someone who cares about you.

Sally   I know. I'm just not sure who I can trust any more. My boyfriend said he was a virgin. But, he couldn't have been or I wouldn't have become infected.

Doctor That's right. Sexually-transmitted infections are contagious. Your boyfriend un- doubtedly had sex with someone who was infected and he passed it on to you.

Sally   It's not fair. We only did it once. He lied to me. I'm not sure if I can ever trust a boy again.

Doctor It is probably a good idea not to be so free with your trust. However, you need to trust someone enough to talk to and sort through your values and your feelings.

Sally   I just can't talk to my mom. She still thinks that I'm her little girl. I'm a teenager. I have feelings—sexual feelings.

Doctor Your mother was a teenager once. And I'm sure she remembers something of what it felt like.

Sally   It's just that she is so judgmental. She has an opinion about everything. She doesn't listen to me, she just jumps to conclusions the minute I begin to talk.

Doctor Do you try to talk to her when she is busy, or do you take her aside and let her know you would really like to have a mother/daughter talk.

Sally I guess I sometimes corner her when she says she doesn't have time.

Doctor What would happen if you made an appointment with her to have a talk? Say something like, "Mom, I have something real important to talk to you about. Can you set aside some time this evening when we can talk?"

Processing Questions

1. Should parents be told when their teenager is diagnosed with a sexually-transmitted infection?
2. Are there any conditions when parents should be told about the sexual activity of their teenagers?
3. Is it possible for parents to be unaware that their teenagers are sexually active?
4. What prevents sexually active teenagers from taking appropriate measures to protect themselves?
5. Whose responsibility is it to provide adequate protection during sexual activity?
6. What are some of the myths concerning protection? When do you need it?
7. At what age should you have the legal responsibility for giving others permission to have sex with you?
8. What reasons do you have for not engaging in sexual activity as a teen?

Discussion Notes

It just isn't fair. Sexual activity is pleasurable; why does it have to come with such serious penalties if misused? Sexually-transmitted infections, unwanted pregnancies, and broken hearts are some of the consequences of having sex prior to establishing a legal and lasting relationship. Parents, teachers, and other adults are often considered "old fashioned" by counseling abstinence until marriage. Discuss some of the reasons your teens have for not becoming sexually active at this time.

Part III
Legalities and Moralities

17   I'm Not a Thief

Subject   Stealing

Setting   A convenience store

Props   Candy bar

Cast   Chad and Jerry

Synopsis   Chad asks Jerry to loan him some money to buy a candy bar. Since Jerry doesn't have any money with him, Chad just steals the candy. Chad doesn't feel that lifting a little candy bar makes him a thief.

Chad   Hey, Jerry. Do you have a dollar I could borrow to get this candy bar?

Jerry   No. I forgot my wallet at home.

Chad   That's okay, I'll just slip it in my pocket and nobody will notice.

Jerry   But what if we get caught? We could get into a lot of trouble.

Chad   We won't get caught. Nobody will even see us.

Jerry   Well, why do you want the candy bar anyway?

Chad   To eat, what do you think?

Jerry   Well I just don't think that it's right for you to be stealing.

Chad   Nobody cares if I take this candy bar. This store makes enough money. They won't care if one little candy bar is missing.

Jerry   Well I care.

Chad   Why? It's not your problem.

Jerry   I care about you. I don't want a thief for a friend.

Chad   Hey, lifting a little bar doesn't make me a thief.

Jerry   Are you sure about that?

Processing Questions

1. Is shoplifting really stealing?
2. Would you loan money to a friend? If so, how much?
3. What does it feel like to *not* have any money?
4. Have you done something inappropriate and then tried to justify it with some pretty shaky logic?
5. How would you feel if you discovered that someone had stolen something from you?
6. Would you try to get even if someone took advantage of you?
7. Are there some things that your friends do that you wish you could change?
8. Have you ever taken a risk or done something simply for the thrill involved?

Discussion Notes

Trust and honesty are very desirable character traits. Sometimes situations occur that reveal our true nature to our friends. While stealing a candy bar may not be considered a major crime, it does reveal a person's values. If it is "no big deal" to steal a candy bar, what would you have to steal for it to be "a big deal?" What if your friend stole from you? Some people engage in inappropriate social behavior simply because of the risk in–volved. A person might shoplift for the thrill of it, not because the object is needed or even desired. This discussion could be expanded to include the need to take risks and how to take socially acceptable risks rather than inappropriate ones.

Don L. Sorenson, Ph.D. with David A. Nord

18   Embarrassing Theft

Subject   Peer helping

Setting   Counseling/peer helper room at school

Props   Table with two chairs

Cast   Peer helper and Mike

Synopsis   Mike was too embarrassed to purchase something he wanted, so he shop-lifted it. He is experiencing guilt for having behaved as he did, but he isn't sure how to handle it, so he talks to a peer helper.

Peer Hi, Mike. How can I help you?

Mike You're a peer helper, right?

Peer That's right.

Mike And I can tell you anything, right?

Peer That's right. What would you like to tell me?

Mike You aren't supposed to tell anyone what I say, right?

Peer I am here to try to help you with a problem. I won't tell other students what we talk about, but sometimes I have to share it with a counselor, especially if someone might be hurt if I don't.

Mike Nobody's going to get hurt. I just don't want other people to know.

Peer You've done something that is embarrassing to you?

Mike No, just something stupid.

Peer Your friends would think it was stupid?

Mike Yeah. I stole something from a store.

Peer It was stupid to steal, or was what you took was stupid?

Mike Both. I stole a package of condoms. I wanted them real bad, but I was afraid to just buy them.

Peer You would have been embarrassed to have the clerk see what you were buying?

Mike I didn't want her to think that I might be having sex.

Peer And are you?

Mike Not yet. But I have been thinking about it.

Peer So you took the condoms to avoid giving the impression that you are sexually active.

Mike Yeah, but now I feel guilty because I stole them. They were only worth about five bucks, but I've never stole anything before in my life.

Peer Your guilt appears to be worse than the embarrassment you thought you would feel by buying the condoms.

Mike I wish I hadn't taken them. I don't know what to do now. It would be too embarrassing to take them back to the store, but I don't like being a thief.

Peer So, what else could you do?

Processing Questions

1. Have you ever been embarrassed to tell someone what it was you wanted to purchase?
2. Why is it important not to have others think bad things about you?
3. Are there some things that are easier to talk about with people your own age?
4. Have you ever talked things over with a peer helper?
5. What does it mean to keep things confidential?
6. If you are a peer helper, when do you refer someone to a counselor or other adult?
7. What do we mean when we say we *feel* guilty?
8. How can you undo a wrong?

Discussion Notes

As sexually developing individuals, teens are torn between wanting to explore these new feelings and fearing being labeled or judged by others. It might seem easier to just steal something like a package of condoms rather than have others see you purchasing them, until guilt sets in. Sex is not something most teens choose to discuss with adults.

Peer helpers are students who are trained listeners. It is important that teens trust these helpers to maintain a confidence, unless, of course, keeping the confidence puts someone in danger. The discussion might be broadened to talking about what types of problems students would rather discuss with peer helpers than with adults.

19   **False Report**

Subject	Forging grades
Setting	Somewhere on the way home after school
Props	Report card, correction fluid, and a pen
Cast	Brent and Salah
Synopsis	Salah is afraid to show his report card to his dad. Brent's solution is to alter a grade on the card. Brent makes a mess out of Salah's report card, making the situation worse.

Brent   Hey Salah, why so sad?

Salah   I got two Ds on my report card.

Brent   So why is that a problem?

Salah   My dad said that if I get any grades below a C, he wouldn't let me play any video games until I got my grades up.

Brent   So, how is he going to know?

Salah   He'll know when I show him my report card.

Brent   Don't show it to him.

Salah   He knows the quarter ends this week.

Brent   Well, how did you get the two Ds anyway?

Salah   I guess I just slacked off in my English class. And the other one, well, I think I forgot to turn in some assignments in math.

Brent   Maybe you could talk to your teachers and get them to give you an incomplete while you make up some work.

Salah   An incomplete is even worse. If I don't get it made up in ten days, I get an F instead.

Brent   Let me see that report card.

Salah   Here. What are going to do?

Brent   Just a little ink eraser and some magic here and presto, the Ds become Bs.

Salah   Let me see that. What did you do? What a mess! There is no way my dad will believe that those are Bs. Now I'm in real trouble.

Brent   I tried.

Salah   What am I going to do now?

Processing Questions

1. What made Brent feel he had permission to take on Salah's problem?
2. What should Brent's consequences be for attempting to alter Salah's grades?
3. Did Salah have any warning that he might not have a good report card?
4. Is not being able to play video games a reasonable and logical consequence for getting poor grades?
5. How important are grades to you?
6. Do you clearly understand the grading requirements of all of your teachers?
7. Do your teachers give you adequate feedback concerning your performance before your grades come out?
8. Do your parents take advantage of parent-teacher conference times?

Discussion Notes

Although grades are extremely important to some students–some because they are planning to enter college and some because of parental expectations–there can be surprises at grading time. Failing to turn in assignments promptly, to study for tests, and to participate in class discussions can have negative effects on grades. If they are in doubt, students need to ask their teachers to describe their grading processes. Tampering with official grade reports is a serious offense. The time to be concerned about a grade is when there is still time to earn a better one.

20   Not Old Enough

Subject   Buying alcohol

Setting   I: A car parked outside a liquor store; II: Front door of Todd & Jay's house

Props   Two chairs representing the front seat of a car

Cast   Todd, Jay, Jorge, and a Police Officer

Synopsis   Jay tries to get his brother to buy beer for him. After he refuses, Jay asks his brother's friend who agrees to help.

Scene I

Todd   *(sitting in the car)* Hey, little brother, what ya doing?

Jay   Me and my friends are going to a party. Want to come?

Jorge   *(sitting in the passenger seat)* Not with you, tiny.

Jay   Come on, Todd. It'll be fun. Besides, we need a little help getting the alcohol. I've got the money; I just need some–one that's old enough to buy it.

Todd   You want me to get into trouble contributing...?

Jay   How did you get your alcohol when you were my age?

Todd   None of your business.

Jay   So, are you going to do it?

Todd   I don't think so. *(to Jorge)* I've got to run an errand. I'll be right back.

Jorge   Take your time. I'll still be here... doing nothing.

(Todd gets out of the car and leaves. Jay goes around to Jorge' side of the car.)

Jay   Hey, Jorge, how about it? There is an extra ten bucks in it if you will get us a bottle of vodka and Bacardi.

Jorge   Well, I guess. I'm not doing anything anyway.

Scene II

(A police officer knocks on the house door. Todd opens the door.)

Officer   Good evening, sir. Do you have a younger brother named Jay?

Todd   Why, officer? Did something happen?

Officer   Is Jay your brother?

Todd   Yes. What's wrong?

Officer   I've got your brother out in my car. He and a couple of his peers were tipping over trash cans. They took off when they saw my squad car. The others got away, but your brother apparently was more intoxi–cated. Do you have any idea how he got the alcohol?

Processing Questions

1. Why do we have age requirements for the purchase of alcohol and cigarettes?
2. How easy is it for teenagers to get alcohol?
3. What is the penalty for purchasing alcohol for minors?
4. What are some other ways young people obtain alcohol?
5. How does a person's behavior change under the influence of alcohol?
6. If you are at a party where alcohol is served, but you do not drink, can you still get into trouble?
7. What do you do if someone offers alcohol to you?
8. What are some things you can do to have fun that do not require the use of alcohol?

Discussion Notes

Most teenagers report that it is not difficult to obtain alcohol. A common method is to have an older brother, sister, or friend make the purchase. While these individuals often are willing to oblige, they are placing themselves at risk for criminal prosecution. The person obtaining the alcohol for a minor also may be liable for any damage caused by the teenagers who are under the influence. Teens sometime argue that if alcohol is legal for adults, it also should be legal for them.

21   Drugs or No?

Subject   Drug abuse
Setting   A place where a group gets together after school
Props   No props required
Cast   Julio, Steve, Kent, and Mike
Synopsis   Mike was observed behaving strangely the night before. His friends con–
             front him regarding his behavior.

Julio Did you see Mike last night? He was high on something.

Steve He was sure enjoying himself.

Kent Yeah, he didn't seem to care who saw him. I hope his dad doesn't find out.

(Mike enters.)

Mike Hey, guys. What's up?

Julio Nothing. We were just talking. By the way, what was up with you last night?

Mike Why?

Steve Seemed like you were acting a little strange. What were you on?

Mike The good stuff, I guess. I don't remember everything, but I was sure feeling good.

Kent It showed.

Mike You guys ever thought of trying it?

Julio I've thought about it, but I don't think it is worth it.

Mike It doesn't cost that much. I can get you a sample cheap.

Julio I wasn't talking of that kind of cost.

Mike What? Are you scared?

Steve He's not scared. He's just not that stupid.

Mike So, you're saying I'm stupid?

Julio No! But, what you are doing is stupid. We all saw how you acted last night. Maybe if you could see yourself when you are high, you wouldn't think that getting high was so great.

Mike But I like it when I am high.

Steve Well, we don't like to be around you when you get like you did last night.

Kent You've got to make a choice, Mike. If you want to hang around us, you've got to leave the drugs alone. It's your choice. What will it be?

Processing Questions

1. What do you think Mike will choose? Drugs or his friends?
2. If you were behaving inappropriately, would your friends confront you?
3. People who use drugs tell themselves things to justify their use. What are some of those things?
4. Are drugs easy to find at your school?
5. What costs are there to drug use, besides the obvious one of money?
6. Knowing all we know about drug abuse, why do people still experiment?
7. Are there any circumstances in which you would accept an offer to "try" an illegal drug?
8. If our school was to undertake a "war on drugs," what are some of the steps we would take?

Discussion Notes

Depending on the statistics you use, drug use is either on the rise or decline among high school students. Some people like to limit a discussion of illegal drug use to pharmacological prod–ucts, while others readily admit that cigarettes and alcohol are the more serious drugs of choice for teens.

Teens are usually well aware of the negative effects of drug use, while still choosing to experiment. Although it is a sensitive area, a discussion on feelings of self–worth and acceptance by others will probably be the most productive way to encourage students to consider abstaining from using harmful and illegal products.

 Don L. Sorenson, Ph.D. with David A. Nord

22   Metered Parking

Subject   Parking and petting

Setting   In Tyler's car

Props   Four chairs to simulate a car

Cast   Tyler, Jonni, Rex, and Teresa

Synopsis   Tyler pulls over so he can make out with his girlfriend, Jonni. Rex tries to follow Tyler's lead, but Teresa, sitting beside him, wants to go home. Teresa feels things are moving too fast, so she asks Tyler to take her home.

Tyler Let's pull over and park for a few minutes.

Jonni You guys doing okay back there?

Rex We're fine. Right, Teresa?

Teresa Sure. But don't stay too long, Tyler. I really need to get home soon.

Tyler Aw, come on. It's a great night. Let's not ruin it.

Jonni Come over here, Tyler.

Rex What's the matter? You're acting kind of strange, Teresa.

Teresa It's getting late. I really should be getting home.

Rex Come on, relax. What will Tyler and Jonni think? I told them you were a cool person. We can't ruin the evening for them.

Teresa I just don't feel comfortable.

Rex Just put your head on my shoulder.

Teresa That's not what I mean. I think I know what you expect of me, but I don't know you well enough yet.

Rex But, that's why we're here–to get to know each other better.

Teresa But, it's moving too fast. This is our first date. Jonni and Tyler have been together for almost a year.

Rex Teresa, I really like you. And here we are. It's a nice night. The moon is full. Let's not talk any more. Come on.

Teresa Tyler, I really need to get home. Can we just go now?

Jonni Oh come on Teresa, just chill out. We're just getting warmed up.

Teresa Please, Tyler. I'm sorry if I'm spoiling your evening. But, I need to get home.

Tyler Come on, Teresa. Rex, can't you do anything with her?

Processing Questions

1. What should you do if you and your date have different expectations for the evening?
2. What types of things should be decided in advance before going on a date?
3. Do you and your friends generally have a plan or do you just "drive around?"
4. Have you ever found yourself in an uncomfortable situation in which you have little or no control?
5. Do you have a plan if you need to escape from an uncomfortable situation?
6. What are some of the pitfalls of double dating?
7. Do you send mixed messages to your friends in certain situations?
8. Are your friends expected to be home at the same time as you are on school nights?

Discussion Notes

Turning sixteen is a milestone for most teens. It means getting to use a car and having an opportunity to drive around with your friends. It also means having a private place, away from parents and teachers, to enjoy the company of peers. Most parents have given their teens some guidelines on how to handle situations in which they might not be totally comfortable. A discussion on ways to extricate yourself from such situations may be beneficial to those who have not thought about them.

23   I Own Her

Subject   Possessive boyfriend

Setting   Casual setting where friends gather and talk

Props   None required

Cast   Steve and Rachel

Synopsis   Steve believes that having a girlfriend means that he owns her and can do whatever he wishes. Rachel advocates for better treatment for Molly, Steve's girlfriend.

Steve   She's my girlfriend, and I can do anything I want.

Rachel   You don't own her.

Steve   Yes, I do. I take care of her, and she's mine. I say what she can do and when she can do it. So, stay out of it.

Rachel   Steve, girls aren't property. You own your car, so I guess you can wreck it if you want to, but you don't own Molly.

Steve   My car, my girlfriend. There's no difference. She's mine and I say what she can do and can't.

Rachel   We don't live in the dark ages. Women have been liberated. Molly is a person and she has rights.

Steve   Molly isn't complaining so why are you?

Rachel   She's probably afraid to tell you anything. You come on so strong. Maybe she's afraid you'll hurt her.

Steve   She wants to be with me. I take good care of her. She'll be fine as long as she does what I tell her to do when I tell her.

Rachel   That's the point. People should be *asked* if they want to do something, not *told* that they have to.

Steve   I expect my girlfriend to do what I tell her to. Besides, a man is supposed to be in charge. Women are just there to make us happy.

Rachel   Are you ever out of it. Slavery is dead. You're lucky to have Molly, but if you don't wake up, someday she won't be there for you.

Steve   She better not leave me.

Rachel   And if she does?

Steve   I'll be mad. No I'd be pissed.

Rachel   Would you go after her?

Steve   Damn right! She's my girl as long as I say she is.

Rachel   Do you think that's the way Molly feels?

Educational Media Corporation®, Box 21311, Minneapolis, MN 55421-0311

Processing Questions

1. Where does Steve get the idea that he has special rights over Molly?
2. What has Molly done to give Steve the feeling that he owns her?
3. In what ways does Molly fear Steve?
4. What makes it hard for Molly to tell her friends how she feels?
5. Does having sex make it easier or harder for two people to express their feelings to each other?
6. What should be at the core of a relationship between two people?
7. Is it difficult for you when you see your friends in unhappy relationships?

Discussion Notes

Anyone who has watched daytime television has seen disgusting characters who claim that their girlfriends are their property. When it involves our friends, it might be difficult to realize that the way some boys treat their girlfriends does not indicate a lot of respect. Fears of being rejected or deserted can cause some girls to tolerate behavior from a "supposed" boyfriend that others would perceive as unhealthy. Relationships need to be continually examined so that they remain based on mutual respect.

Session IV
Home and Family

24   Private Eyes

Subject   Privacy at home

Setting   Any place students gather after school

Props   None required

Cast   Tony, Rick, and Wes

Synopsis   Tony is disturbed that he has no private space at home. He suspects that his mother is going through his things because she doesn't trust him.

Tony A man's home is his castle, right?

Rick I've heard that.

Wes In my case it is more like a shoebox.

Tony What do you mean?

Wes All I have that is mine would fit into a shoebox. I've got a brother and two sisters. I have to share a bedroom and I have zero privacy.

Tony Well, I don't have to share a bedroom, but I don't have any privacy either.

Rick Why not?

Tony My mom. You'd think that by the time you are sixteen, she would leave me alone and stay out of my room. I know she snoops in everything when I am gone.

Wes How do you know?

Tony She moves things around on my desk.

Wes Does she clean your room or make your bed?

Tony Yeah, she's always picking things up. I can't find any–thing.

Wes Be thankful! If anything gets cleaned in my room, it's me or my brother. My mom wouldn't lift a finger, even if the garbage got to be three feet deep in there.

Rick I wouldn't like that. I don't mind if my mom comes into my room, but I would be really mad if I thought she were looking through my stuff–like she didn't trust me.

Tony Do you think she has ever looked through your stuff?

Rick I don't think so. She respects my privacy. And I respect her privacy.

Tony I'm not sure if my mom trusts me or not, but I wish she would respect my privacy. How can I get her to leave my stuff alone?

Processing Questions

1. Is there any place in your home that you consider your private place?
2. Do you think your parents have a right to search your room?
3. Are you responsible for keeping your room clean?
4. Have you ever left something in your room that you wanted a parent to find?
5. Do you have to earn the trust of others?
6. What have you done to build trust with your parents?
7. How do parents transfer responsibility to their children?
8. How much should a teenager be responsible for?

Discussion Notes

Parents are legally responsible for the behavior of their children. However, teenagers do not become responsible for their own behavior simply because they pass a certain birthday. Responsibility has to be learned–transferred slowly to the teen according to his or her ability to handle it. Parents differ in their willingness to transfer certain responsibilities to their children. It might be helpful to compare the different ranges of responsibility given to teens by different parents. Perhaps, if we are not doing anything that we are ashamed of, we are not as concerned about privacy.

25   Bad Connection

Subject   Hiding liquor at home

Setting   Nick's basement bedroom

Props   Partially full liquor bottle, chair to stand on

Cast   Lori and Rick, Nick's parents

Synopsis   Nick's dad is stringing a video cable through the drop ceiling in Nicks's basement bedroom. He discovers an open bottle of liquor. Nick's mother is afraid of how his father will confront Nick about the liquor.

Lori Rick, what are you doing on that chair?

Rick I'm stringing this cable so we can connect the TV in our bedroom to the dish.

Lori That's great! What took you so long to think of that?

Rick I get tired of just listening to you snore when I can't sleep.

Lori And you think I am the only one who snores?

Rick Well, now you will have something else to listen to if you can't sleep.

Lori Just be careful. Don't fall down!

Rick Lori, there is something up here.

Lori What is it, Rick?

Rick Look here. (*Shows her a bottle of liquor.*)

Lori What is it?

Rick It's booze.

Lori How did it get there?

Rick Well, since it was over Nick's bed, I'm betting he put it there.

Lori I wonder where he got it?

Rick It doesn't matter where he got it. The problem is that he has it. He's knows how we feel about this stuff.

Lori You'd better have a talk with him.

Rick I'll do more than talk.

Lori What are you going to do?

Processing Questions

1. What expectations do you have for privacy at home?
2. How important is it for you to have your own bedroom?
3. Do you have anything stashed at your house that you would not like your parents to find?
4. What are some of the reasons that society has made the purchase and use of alcohol illegal for teenagers?
5. What penalty would be appropriate for Nick?
6. Is there anything you do that you would not like to become public?
7. Are there any times when it is appropriate to experiment with the consumption of alcohol?
8. Do your parents feel comfortable discussing important topics with you?

Discussion Notes

When Tyler asked to have a bedroom in the basement, he was counting on the fact that he would have his own room away from the center of family activity. The moveable ceiling tiles provided a perfect place to keep private things out of reach from little brothers, and away from the prying eyes of parents. It is hard to anticipate everything, especially the fact that things you intended to keep private might become public. It could be said that if you don't have anything to hide, then you are not worried about something being discovered. This discussion could be expanded from hiding things to hiding behaviors.

26   **And Baby Makes Three**

Subject	Baby sitting blues
Setting	I. Somewhere in Terra's house; II. Later that evening
Props	None required
Cast	Mom, Terra, Jason, and Emily (young sister going to bed)
Synopsis	Her mom asks Terra to babysit so she can go out. Terra wants to have Jason over if she has to stay home. Against her mother's orders, she invites Jason to come over anyway.

Scene I

Mom I am going to be gone tonight. Can you watch Emily?

Terra Mom, I had to stay home and babysit last night.

Mom Just let her watch TV while you do your homework and put her to bed at 8:00 p.m.

Terra Then can Jason come over?

Mom You know how I feel about that. I don't want anyone else in the house when I am not here.

Terra Mom, I need a life, too.

Mom There is plenty of time for that later. The next thing you know you will be pregnant and raising kids. Don't be in a hurry.

Terra It's not fair. You get to go out and have a good time and I'm stuck here alone.

Mom You're not alone. Emily's here.

Terra But, Mom, Emily is your re–sponsibility, not mine.

Mom You are both my responsibil–ity. No one in the house when I am not home. That's final!

Scene II

(Later that evening)

Terra No more stories. It is time to go to sleep. Good night, Emily.

Jason Do you think she will stay in there?

Terra She will. Besides, we can go into my mom's room.

Jason Did your mom say it was okay for me to come over?

Terra She doesn't care what I do. All she's interested in is having a good time.

Jason I'm all for a good time, too.

Terra Mom says it's a real drag having a couple of kids to take care of. I guess she's glad that I'm old enough to babysit. She said it was pretty tough being a single mom when I was little and Emily was a baby.

Jason Where was your dad?

Terra He disappeared just after Emily was born. I haven't seen him since.

Jason How could anyone do that? I couldn't leave my girl, even if she did have a couple of rug rats running around.

Terra Rug rats! Is that what you think about kids?

Jason I guess I don't think much about kids. It's a little soon to be thinking about taking on the responsibility of a family. I just want to be close to the woman I love. And that's you.

Terra I imagine that's how my dad felt, too, once...

Jason Let's not get ahead of ourselves, now. This is getting too heavy. We've got the evening–and the house pretty much to ourselves. What do you say we go into your mom's bedroom?

Processing Questions

1. Are parents within their rights to limit guests when they are not home?
2. Do you have a right to refuse to babysit a younger sibling?
3. How do you communicate with parents who are separated?
4. What arrangements can you make with a single parent to share responsibilities and time out?
5. How can you support your single parents when they have personal needs?
6. Does taking responsibility for a younger sibling make you feel older than you are and, therefore, entitled to adult privileges?
7. Would having to share a parenting role (taking care of a younger sibling) with a single parent discourage you from starting a family?

Discussion Notes

Single parent families are more common than ever. This usually results in older children being pressed into assisting with the upbringing of younger children–sometimes even while the parent is dating. When both parent and teenager are dating at the same time, conflicts are bound to result. Told that they are old enough to be responsible for younger siblings, they might also believe that they are old enough to enjoy adult freedoms. A discussion of how to balance rights and responsibilities could produce some clarity as to what are reasonable and proper expectations.

27   **Who Cares?**

Subject	Home alone
Setting	I. Zack's house; Juan on another phone on the other side of the stage; II. Later that evening
Props	Two phones, refrigerator with beer, video tapes
Cast	Zack, Juan, Diane, and Evelyn
Synopsis	Zack has the house to himself so he invites some friends over. Dad is supposed to be pretty cool about things, having beer in the refrigerator and X-rated videos. Evelyn is reluctant to get involved.

Scene I

Zack *(on the phone)* Are you doing anything tonight?

Juan *(on the phone)* Why? What's happening?

Zack I got the house to myself tonight. Come on over. Dad's got the place pretty well stocked.

Juan Mind if I bring a couple of friends?

Zack No problem.

Juan Okay. See ya soon.

Scene II

(Diane, Evelyn and Juan enter.)

Diane Hi, Zack.

Zack Come on in. Make yourself comfortable. Drinks are in the fridge.

Diane Beer! Great!

Juan Help yourself. His dad doesn't care.

Zack Nah. My dad's pretty cool about things. Besides, he's gone for the rest of the night.

Diane Got any videos?

Zack Sure. There's a big stack over there. Take your pick.

Diane *(checking video titles)* Oh! Wow! Some goood stuff here! Your dad's private collection?

Zack He doesn't care what I watch.

Juan Looks like porn to me.

Diane We're not kids. Let's put one in.

Evelyn When is your dad coming back?

Zack Probably not until late. Anyway, he doesn't care.

Evelyn I know. You've said that several times. But, shouldn't we care?

Processing Questions

1. What are some of the dangers of inviting others over when there is no parental supervision?

2. Do your parents have any requirements concerning visiting the homes of friends?

3. What should you say or do if you find yourself in a situation in which you are not comfortable?

4. In the absence of a caring parent, what keeps you from stepping out of bounds?

5. Do you secretly wish that your parents *would* object to some of the things you do?

6. Why would parents object to having their teens exposed to pornographic videos and literature?

7. With pornographic materials advertised and available on the internet, what keeps you from exploring these things?

8. How much of our values are transferred to us by our parents?

Discussion Notes

Most parents respect the laws and morals of society. Most parents withhold alcohol and sexually-explicit materials from their minor children, but some believe it is okay for their teens to experience these things, especially if they are in the privacy of their own homes. Although they may believe they are not encouraging these things, they do nothing to discourage or prohibit the things society has made unlawful. Behavior is usually controlled in two ways, by *shame*–fear of being caught and ridiculed by others–or *guilt*–knowing that a particular behavior is contrary to one's internalized values. Without internal values of right and wrong, we are controlled only by shame, which is usually insufficient to keep us on a strong, healthy path.

28   Happy Hour for Dad

Subject   Alcoholic parent

Setting   Gina's family living room or kitchen

Props   None required

Cast   Mom and Gina

Synopsis   Mom learns that Gina is unwillling to invite friends over to her house because of her dad's drinking problem. Her mom wants to know more about her friends and to have Gina feel comfortable at home. So, what do they do about Dad?

Gina Mom, can I spend the night at Mary's?

Mom Why don't you ever ask any- one to spend the night here?

Gina I'd like to, but I just never know about Dad.

Mom I know he has his problem with alcohol, but he doesn't hurt anybody.

Gina I know that but, I'm afraid he'll embarrass me.

Mom You know, I never get a chance to see any of your friends.

Gina I just don't feel comfortable having kids over.

Mom But, this is your house, too.

Gina Dad doesn't seem to think so.

Mom What do you mean?

Gina He doesn't seem to care whether I am here or not, and he never asks me about my friends or what I'm doing.

Mom Well, I care about you, and I want to know more about you and your friends.

Gina So, what are we going to do about Dad?

Processing Questions

1. Are you comfortable having friends visit your home?
2. Is there anything about your parents' behavior that you would like to see changed?
3. How can you get help coping and living with an alcoholic parent?
4. Do you like visiting a particular friend's home? What is special about that home?
5. How well do your parents know your friends?
6. What can you do if you have an unsupportive parent?
7. What do you do to make your home an inviting place for your friends?

Discussion Notes

Home may be "where the heart its," but it also can be a place that you feel uncomfortable sharing with friends. The behavior of a parent, a lack of private space, or your family's economic status are just a few reasons why you might be reluctant to entertain your friends in your home. Although it could be easy to get sidetracked discussing the singular issue of coping with an alcoholic parent, the broader issue of what it takes to feel comfortable enough about one's home to share it with friends should be the focus.

If friends cannot be welcomed into your home, discuss ways to involve supportive parents with your friends outside of the home. Parents can chaperone dances, class activities, and school trips, to mention just a few possibilities.

29   **Skinny Dipping**

Subject   Physical abuse

Setting   A meeting place outside school

Props   None required

Cast   Jeana, Lora, and Carole

Synopsis   Lora's friends have been invited to go swimming in the new pool at Mary's. Lora pretends that she has a rash and doesn't want others to see it, when, in fact, she has some bumps and bruises from some abuse inflicted at home.

Jeana   Hey, Lora. A few of us are going over to Mary's. They have a new pool. How about coming along?

Lora   I don't think so.

Carole   Why not? You do swim, don't you?

Lora   Yeah. But, I've got a... a rash and it looks kind of ugly.

Jeana   What's a little rash? Besides, there won't be any boys there–just us girls.

Lora   Well...

Carole   Come on. We'll go by your house so you can grab your suit. We'll put them on at Mary's.

Lora   Okay, but I'll put my suit on at home first.

Jeana   I didn't know you're so shy.

Lora   I'm not, normally. I just don't want to show off my... my rash.

Carole   I don't understand you, Lora. This isn't like you.

Lora   Just drop it, okay?

Jeana   Something is going on here that we don't understand. Is there something more than a rash that you don't want us to see?

Lora   I just don't want to get you two involved, that's all.

Carole   We're friends, Lora. If there is something wrong, we want to help you.

Jeana   Yeah, that's what friends are for.

Lora   I've got some... bruises and bumps on my back. They don't hurt, but they don't look too good either.

Carole   How did you get them?

Lora   I did something wrong and my dad punished me. Please don't tell anybody, okay?

Jeana   But, that's not right. There must be something that we can do to help.

Carole   Any ideas?

Processing Questions

1. Why are some teens unwilling to tell others about parental abuse?
2. What help is available to a teen being abused by a parent?
3. Is there ever a time when a parent is justified in using physical punishment?
4. Are there more effective ways for parents to discipline their teenagers?
5. What distinguishes justifiable punishment from abuse?
6. Is the reverse possible, teens physically abusing their parents?
7. Could there be another reason why Lora wouldn't want to change at a friend's house?

Discussion Notes

While parents have the responsibility to discipline their minor children, they do not have the right to physically abuse them. What may begin as spankings when the child is young can escalate to more physical punishment as the child gets older, if the parent believes in corporal punishment. Parents need to use something other than physical punishment to control behavior. Students might benefit from discussing discipline methods their parents use that are acceptable and not abusive.

30   Family Vacation

Subject   Family obligations
Setting   A gathering place for friends
Props   None required
Cast   Robert, Jed, and Marco
Synopsis   Robert's family is planning to take a family vacation by car and he doesn't want to go. His dad makes all the plans and dictates that everyone partici-pate.

Robert   You ever see *National Lampoon's Family Vacation?*

Jed   You mean that movie with Chevy Chase in it?

Robert   Yeah. Well, guess what?

Jed   What?

Robert   My family is planning a family vacation, and I have to go along.

Marco   Are you flying to Wally World?

Robert   No, I wish. We're going to drive across country. Five of us in a car made for four.

Jed   Sounds like this vacation is going to bring your family real close together.

Robert   Too close. I don't even get along with my younger brother and sister. When we are in the car, even for a short ride, their hands are all over each other. My dad yells at my mom to get them to stop, but they just keep on doing it. It gets really annoying.

Marco   But, wont it be fun to get out of this boring little town for a while?

Robert   I guess so, but I wish I had a vote in deciding where we are going.

Jed   Where are you going?

Robert   My dad hasn't said yet. I was hoping we might get to go to St. Louis. They have a Six Flags there.

Marco   Have you told him where you want to go?

Robert   Do you think my family is a democracy? We go where my dad says we're going.

Jed   Does your mom have any-thing to say about it?

Robert   I don't think so. I've never heard her opinion.

Marco   That would be tough not to have someone listen to my feelings and opinions.

Jed   There must be something you could do to get your two cents in.

Robert   Like what?

Processing Questions

1. Are there things that you are required to do with your family that you dislike?
2. Do you have any input into your family vacation plans?
3. What would be your ideal vacation?
4. How could you contribute to making your dream vacation a reality?
5. Does your family discuss family problems, concerns, and decisions?
6. What do you do with members of your family that is fun?
7. Which member of your family are you closest to?
8. Given a choice, is there someone in your family that you would rather not spend time with?

Discussion Notes

Families are the basic units of our society. Some of our fondest childhood memories should be of the things we did as a family. As we get older, the interests we share with younger siblings change. Parents want to do things as a family, but they often are unaware of which activities their children consider to be fun. Family meetings are one way to improve communication and involve children in family decisions. Discuss how one might go about establishing a time when the family meets and what rules (i.e., each has a vote, no put downs, etc.) should prevail at those times.

31   Visiting Aunt Mary

Subject	Family obligations
Setting	The kitchen in Sam's house
Props	None required
Cast	Sam and his mom
Synopsis	Sam's mom wants him to come along to visit his elderly Aunt Mary in a nursing home. She hopes that the trip will give her a chance to catch up on what is happening in Sam's life.

Sam   Do I have to go?

Mom   You know how much Aunt Mary likes you.

Sam   She doesn't even know me any more. The last time I went to see her, she completely ignored me.

Mom   She's not always like that. Sometimes she has good days. Last time I saw her, we had a great conversation.

Sam   But, I hate nursing homes. They smell bad. And all those old people just stare at me.

Mom   They are probably thinking what a fine young man you are. And, how good you are to visit your Aunt.

Sam   But, I had plans.

Mom   I really don't want to drive all that way alone. Besides, I might even let you drive part of the way.

Sam   That's bribery, Mom. You know I need all the practice I can get before I take my test.

Mom   Then, you'll go?

Sam   Can I bring a friend along?

Mom   I was kind of hoping that it would just be a family day. I don't get to spend much time with you any more.

Sam   Mom, you see me every day.

Mom   But, we don't seem to have any time to talk.

Sam   What do you want to talk about?

Mom   Maybe I'd just like to know a little bit more about what's going on in your life.

Sam   Nothing really. School, home-work, and hanging out with my friends.

Mom   So, would it be so hard to come with me to see Aunt Mary on Saturday–just the two of us?

Processing Questions

1. Why is it difficult to visit the elderly?

2. Is there someone in your extended family that would enjoy a visit from you?

3. Can you picture yourself and what you will be like at the age of 65?

4. Are you asked to do some things by your parents that you really don't want to do?

5. Can you be bribed to do something that is displeasing to you?

6. Even though you see your parents every day, do they really know what is happening in your life?

7. How well do you feel your parents know you and how you spend your time?

8. Do you have times that you spend alone with one of your parents?

Discussion Notes

We all get old, but when you are a teenager, old age doesn't seem like a personal reality. Aging relatives lose their appeal as they are no longer the individuals that interacted with you when you were young. You prefer to spend time with your friends; even your parents become a little more irrelevant as you experience the new mobility and freedom of being a teen. A discussion of what your presence means to adults, even parents, might cause them to look at spending some time with their parents and the elderly as not being so painful.

Part V
The 21st Century

The following energizers and icebreakers are available from Educational Media Corporation®, PO Box 21311, Minneapolis, MN 55421 (1–800–966–3382).

Foster, E.S. (1989, 1998). *Energizers and icebreakers.* Minneapolis, MN: Educational Media Corporation.

Foster–Harrison, E. (1994). *More energizers and icebreakers.* Minneapolis, MN: Educational Media Corporation.

Hazouri, S.P., & McLaughlin, M.S. (1993). *Warm ups & wind downs.* Minneapolis, MN: Educational Media Corporation.

Olson, C. (2000) *Energizers: Calisthenics for the mind.* Minneapolis, MN: Educational Media Corporation.

Tubesing, N.L. (1997). *Instant icebreakers.* Duluth, MN: Whole Person Associates.

West, E. (1997). *201 icebreakers.* New York, NY: McGraw–Hill.

West, E. (1999). *The big book of icebreakers.* New York, NY: McGraw–Hill.

32   September 11, 2001

Subject   Terrorist attack or threat

Setting   The school parking lot in the middle of the school day. A stiff wind is blow-
             ing and it is cold.

Props   Coats to represent the cold, outside weather

Cast   Hope, Chris, and Martin

Synopsis   The school building has been evacuated due to a bomb threat. Students are
             not happy having their routines interrupted with threats of violence.

Hope   I can't believe this is happen-
           ing here. This isn't New York
           or Washington.

Chris Why shouldn't it happen
           here? Are we surrounded by
           some bubble that protects us?

Hope   No, but it's something that
           usually happens someplace
           else.

Martin Well, it's happened here.
           Somebody called in a bomb
           threat and that's why we are
           standing out here freezing
           our....

Chris I guess we could go home... or
           somewhere. It'll take them
           hours to check the building.

Hope   But, I don't want to go home.
           We were supposed to have
           practice after school. The
           tournament is less than a
           week away and we really need
           to practice.

Martin I'm sure there's not going to
           be any practice today. It's just
           a mess. Lots of things won't
           get done today. Someone
           thought this was a funny
           prank.

Hope   Well, it wasn't very funny. I'm
           so mad! We've got all this
           security here at school–metal
           detectors, private security
           officers, and even I–D badges.
           And still they are able to get
           to us–to screw up our lives.

Chris I don't think things will ever
           be like they were before Sep-
           tember 11th.

Martin It didn't start with September
           11th. Things have been going
           downhill for some time. Did
           you forget Columbine High
           School?

Chris The "bad guys" have been
           messing things up for us for
           some time now.

Martin And we respond by adding
           more security.

Hope   There must be something else
           we can do. It shouldn't have
           to be like this, should it?

Chris No, it shouldn't, but what can
           three kids do?

Processing Questions

1. What penalties are appropriate for students who make bomb threats?

2. Are there certain types of students in your school that evoke fear and distrust? Which types?

3. What can be done to help troubled students express their anger and frustrations in appropriate ways?

4. Does your school have a plan for handling emergencies?

5. What conditions should exist before school administrators clear a building because of a bomb threat?

6. When does something cease to be a prank and become a threat?

7. Is it more likely that terrorism will strike in a big city or in a small one?

8. Do metal detectors, security officers, and I–D badges really make a school safer?

Discussion Notes

September 11, 2001 caused us all to rethink our feelings about security. What results is often an escalation of measures taken to protect and control. There has been much discussion as to whether these methods really improve our security, or just strengthen a perception that we are safer. Many of the threats to security and safety in schools come from the students themselves. Students who feel isolated, alone, and bullied often develop strong enough feelings to cause them to seek revenge on individual students or the school as a whole. Much of the security measures put in place after a tragedy are like locking the barn door after the horse has been stolen. The best method for identifying these students is the students themselves, reporting threats–however insignificant they appear–to school authorities. Students often are reluctant to do this because of the fear of being labeled as a tattletale. Care must be given to protect the sources of information and the rights of students being investigated.

33   **Internet Confidentiality**

Subject	Internet security
Setting	Heather's room at home
Props	Computer
Cast	Heather, Sarah, and Rachael
Synopsis	Heather has a new computer and she is enjoying the chat rooms. Her friends point out that the people she communicates with might not be who they say they are.

Heather   I'm really enjoying my new computer, although my mom has been on my back. She says I spend too much time on it.

Rachael   Maybe you should teach her how to use it. If she knew how much fun it is, maybe she'd want to use it herself.

Heather   Yeah, but she'd probably want to use it when I want to, and then we'd really be at each other.

Sarah   What do you do on the computer all the time, Heather? I've tried to call you several times lately; I just get a busy signal.

Heather   I did some research for my science project. But, what I really enjoy are the chat rooms. The conversations can get pretty interesting.

Sarah   Like what do you talk about?

Heather   Lots of things. There was a girl from California on last night that really has had some interesting experiences. She said she was fourteen years old. I "heard" some things that are a little bit embarrassing to talk about. But, in the chat room it seemed okay to talk about them because we are all strangers.

Rachael   How do you know for sure that she was a fourteen–year–old from California?

Sarah   Or that she was even a girl?

Heather   What do you mean? She said she was.

Rachael   Do you tell who you really are when you sign on?

Heather   Sure. It's supposed to be a chat room for teenage girls.

Sarah   What's to stop a guy from signing on and pretending to be a girl?

Rachael   Or a pervert?

Heather   Why would they do that?

Rachael   Maybe they are hoping that after you loosen up a little bit, that you will let them know who you really are–like your real name, phone number, address, or something.

Heather   Oh, no! I did give my name and e-mail address to someone. She said she wanted to contact me privately about something really important. What do you suppose is going to happen now? What should I do?

Processing Questions

1. Have you ever entered into a chat room pretending you were someone you were not?

2. What is the appeal for communicating via computer with someone you do not know?

3. What should you share about your identity with someone you meet through a chat room?

4. Are there certain subjects that you feel more comfortable discussing anonymously?

5. Is there any time when it would be appropriate to agree to meet someone you met via computer?

6. How much time should be spent on a computer each night?

7. What supervision, if any, do your parents provide concerning your computer usage?

8. What is the biggest positive contribution that computers have made to your life?

Discussion Notes

The computer and the internet have made it possible for us to communicate anonymously with others, being able to discuss subjects that we feel uncomfortable talking about with people who know us. Skillful manipulators of words and feelings have been able to entice unsuspecting chat room participants into face–to–face meetings, often with the purpose of a sexual encounter. Beginning with the relative safety of anonymity in a chat room, the lure of the dare, challenge, or adventure can lead to a dangerous encounter with an unknown person.

Parents are responsible for the safety of their children. They have both a right and a responsibility to monitor computer usage, knowing when to break off communication under suspicious circumstances.